The Right To Ignore The State

by Herbert Spencer

The Right to Ignore the State.

§ 1. As a corollary to the proposition that all institutions must be subordinated to the law of equal freedom, we cannot choose but admit the right of the citizen to adopt a condition of voluntary outlawry. If every man has freedom to do all that he wills, provided he infringes not the equal freedom of any other man, then he is free to drop connection with the State,—to relinquish its protection and to refuse paying towards its support. It is self-evident that in so behaving he in no way trenches upon the liberty of others; for his position is a passive one, and, whilst passive, he cannot become an aggressor. It is equally self-evident that he cannot be compelled to continue one of a political corporation without a breach of the moral law, seeing that citizenship involves payment of taxes; and the taking away of a man's property against his will is an infringement of his rights. Government being simply an agent employed in common by a number of individuals to secure to them certain advantages, the very nature of the connection implies that it is for each to say whether he will employ such an agent or not. If any one of them determines to ignore this mutual-safety confederation, nothing can be said, except that he loses all claim to its good offices, and exposes himself to the danger of maltreatment,—a thing he is quite at liberty to do if he likes. He cannot be coerced into political combination without a breach of the law of equal freedom; he *can* withdraw from it without committing any such breach; and he has therefore a right so to withdraw.

§ 2. "No human laws are of any validity if contrary to the law of nature: and such of them as are valid derive all their force and all their authority mediately or immediately from this original." Thus writes Blackstone, to whom let all honour be given for having so far outseen the ideas of his time,—and, indeed, we may say of our time. A good antidote, this, for those political superstitions which so widely prevail. A good check upon that sentiment of power-worship which still misleads us by magnifying the prerogatives of constitutional governments as it once did those of monarchs. Let men learn that a legislature is *not* "our God upon earth," though, by the authority they ascribe to it and the things they expect from it, they would seem to think it is. Let them learn rather that it is an institution serving a purely temporary purpose, whose power, when not stolen, is, at the best, borrowed.

Nay, indeed, have we not seen that government is essentially immoral? Is it not the offspring of evil, bearing about it all the marks of its parentage? Does it not exist because crime exists? Is it not strong, or, as we say, despotic, when crime is great? Is there not more liberty—that is, less government—as crime diminishes? And must not government cease when crime ceases, for very lack of objects on which to perform its function? Not only does magisterial power exist *because* of evil, but it exists *by* evil. Violence is employed to maintain it; and all violence involves criminality. Soldiers, policemen, and gaolers; swords, batons, and fetters,—are instruments for inflicting pain; and all infliction of pain is, in the abstract, wrong. The State employs evil weapons to subjugate evil, and is alike contaminated by the objects with which it deals and the means by which it works. Morality cannot recognise it; for morality, being simply a statement of the perfect law, can give no countenance to anything growing out of, and living by, breaches of that law. Wherefore legislative authority can never be ethical—must always be conventional merely.

Hence there is a certain inconsistency in the attempt to determine the right position, structure, and conduct of a government by appeal to the first principles of rectitude. For, as just pointed out, the acts of an institution which is, in both nature and origin, imperfect cannot be made to square with the perfect law. All that we can do is to ascertain, firstly, in what attitude a legislature must stand to the community to avoid being by its mere existence an embodied wrong; secondly, in what manner it must be constituted so as to exhibit the least incongruity with the moral law; and, thirdly, to what sphere its actions must be limited to prevent it from multiplying those breaches of equity it is set up to prevent.

The first condition to be conformed to before a legislature can be established without violating the law of equal freedom is the acknowledgment of the right now under discussion—the right to ignore the State.

§ 3. Upholders of pure despotism may fitly believe State-control to be unlimited and unconditional. They who assert that men are made for governments and not governments for men may consistently hold that no one can remove himself beyond the pale of political organisation. But they who maintain that the people are the only legitimate source of power—that legislative authority is not original, but deputed—cannot deny the right to ignore the State without entangling themselves in an absurdity.

For, if legislative authority is deputed, it follows that those from whom it proceeds are the masters of those on whom it is conferred: it follows further that as masters they confer the said authority voluntarily: and this implies that they may give or withhold it as they please. To call that deputed which is wrenched from men whether they will or not is nonsense. But what is here true of all collectively is equally true of each separately. As a government can rightly act for the people only when empowered by them, so also can it rightly act for the individual only when empowered by him. If A, B, and C debate whether they shall employ an agent to perform for them a certain service, and if, whilst A and B agree to do so, C dissents, C cannot equitably be made a party to the agreement in spite of himself. And this must be equally true of thirty as of three: and, if of thirty, why not of three hundred, or three thousand, or three millions?

§ 4. Of the political superstitions lately alluded to, none is so universally diffused as the notion that majorities are omnipotent. Under the impression that the preservation of order will ever require power to be wielded by some party, the moral sense of our time feels that such power cannot rightly be conferred on any but the largest moiety of society. It interprets literally the saying that "the voice of the people is the voice of God," and, transferring to the one the sacredness attached to the other, it concludes that from the will of the people—that is, of the majority—there can be no appeal. Yet is this belief entirely erroneous.

Suppose, for the sake of argument, that, struck by some Malthusian panic, a legislature duly representing public opinion were to enact that all children born during the next ten years should be drowned. Does any one think such an enactment would be warrantable? If not, there is evidently a limit to the power of a majority. Suppose, again, that of two races living together—Celts and Saxons, for example—the most numerous determined to make the others their slaves. Would the authority of the greatest number be in such case valid? If not, there is something to which its authority must be subordinate. Suppose, once more, that all men having incomes under £50 a year were to resolve upon reducing every income above that amount to their own standard, and appropriating the excess for public purposes. Could their resolution be justified? If not, it must be a third time confessed that there is a law to which the popular voice must defer. What, then, is that law, if not the law of pure equity—the law of equal freedom? These restraints, which all would put to the will of the majority, are exactly the restraints set up by that law. We deny the right of a majority to murder, to enslave, or to rob, simply because murder, enslaving, and robbery are violations of that law—violations too gross to be overlooked. But, if great violations of it are wrong, so also are smaller ones. If the will of the many cannot supersede the first principle of morality in these cases, neither can it in any. So that, however insignificant the minority, and however trifling the proposed trespass against their rights, no such trespass is permissible.

When we have made our constitution purely democratic, thinks to himself the earnest reformer, we shall have brought government into harmony with absolute justice. Such a faith, though perhaps needful for the age, is a very erroneous one. By no process can coercion be made equitable. The freest form of government is only the least objectionable form. The rule of the many by the few we call tyranny: the rule of the few by the many is tyranny also, only of a less intense kind. "You shall do as we will, and not as you will," is in either case the declaration; and, if the hundred make it to ninety-nine, instead of the ninety-nine to the hundred, it is only a fraction less immoral. Of two such parties, whichever fulfils this declaration necessarily breaks the law of equal freedom: the only difference being that by the one it is broken in the persons of ninety-nine, whilst by the other it is broken in the persons of a hundred. And the merit of the democratic form of government consists solely in this,—that it trespasses against the smallest number.

The very existence of majorities and minorities is indicative of an immoral state. The man whose character harmonises with the moral law, we found to be one who can obtain complete happiness without diminishing the happiness of his fellows. But the enactment of public arrangements by vote implies a society consisting of men otherwise constituted—implies that the desires of some cannot be satisfied without sacrificing the desires of others—implies that in the pursuit of their happiness the majority inflict a certain amount of *un*happiness on the minority— implies, therefore, organic immorality. Thus, from another point of view, we again perceive that even in its most equitable form it is impossible for government to dissociate itself from evil; and further, that, unless the right to ignore the State is recognised, its acts must be essentially criminal.

§ 5. That a man is free to abandon the benefits and throw off the burdens of citizenship, may indeed be inferred from the admissions of existing authorities and of current opinion. Unprepared as they probably are for so extreme a doctrine as the one here maintained, the Radicals of our day yet unwittingly profess their belief in a maxim which obviously embodies this doctrine. Do we not continually hear them quote Blackstone's assertion that "no subject of England can be constrained to pay any aids or taxes even for the defence of the realm or the support of government, but such as are imposed by his own consent, or that of his representative in Parliament"? And what does this mean? It means, say they, that every man should have a vote. True: but it means much more. If there is any sense in words, it is a distinct enunciation of the very right now contended for. In affirming that a man may not be taxed unless he has directly or indirectly given his consent, it affirms that he may refuse to be so taxed; and to refuse to be taxed is to cut all connection with the State. Perhaps it will be said that this consent is not a specific, but a general, one, and that the citizen is understood to have assented to every thing his representative may do, when he voted for him. But suppose he did not vote for him; and on the contrary did all in his power to get elected some one holding opposite views—what then? The reply will probably be that by taking part in such an election, he tacitly agreed to abide by the decision of the majority. And how if he did not vote at all? Why then he cannot justly complain of any tax, seeing that he made no protest against its imposition. So, curiously enough, it seems that he gave his consent in whatever way he acted—whether he said "Yes," whether he said "No," or whether he remained neuter! A rather awkward doctrine, this. Here stands an unfortunate citizen who is asked if he will pay money for a certain proffered advantage; and, whether he employs the only means of expressing his refusal or does not employ it, we are told that he practically agrees, if only the number of others who agree is greater than the number of those who dissent. And thus we are introduced to the novel principle that A's consent to a thing is not determined by what A says, but by what B may happen to say!

It is for those who quote Blackstone to choose between this absurdity and the doctrine above set forth. Either his maxim implies the right to ignore the State, or it is sheer nonsense.

§ 6. There is a strange heterogeneity in our political faiths. Systems that have had their day, and are beginning here and there to let the daylight through, are patched with modern notions utterly unlike in quality and colour; and men gravely display these systems, wear them, and walk about in them, quite unconscious of their grotesqueness. This transition state of ours, partaking as it does equally of the past and the future, breeds hybrid theories exhibiting the oddest union of bygone despotism and coming freedom. Here are types of the old organisation curiously disguised by germs of the new— peculiarities showing adaptation to a preceding state modified by rudiments that prophesy of something to come—making altogether so chaotic a mixture of relationships that there is no saying to what class these births of the age should be referred.

As ideas must of necessity bear the stamp of the time, it is useless to lament the contentment with which these incongruous beliefs are held. Otherwise it would seem unfortunate that men do not pursue to the end the trains of reasoning which have led to these partial modifications. In the present case, for example, consistency would force them to admit that, on other points besides the one just noticed, they hold opinions and use arguments in which the right to ignore the State is involved.

For what is the meaning of Dissent? The time was when a man's faith and his mode of worship were as much determinable by law as his secular acts; and, according to provisions extant in our statute-book, are so still. Thanks to the growth of a Protestant spirit, however, we have ignored the State in this matter—wholly in theory, and partly in practice. But how have we done so? By assuming an attitude which, if consistently maintained, implies a right to ignore the State entirely. Observe the positions of the two parties. "This is your creed," says the legislator; "you must believe and openly profess what is here set down for you." "I shall not do anything of the kind," answers the Nonconformist; "I will go to prison rather." "Your religious ordinances," pursues the legislator, "shall be such as we have prescribed. You shall attend the churches we have endowed, and adopt the ceremonies used in them." "Nothing shall induce me to do so," is the reply; "I altogether deny your power to dictate to me in such matters, and mean to resist to the uttermost." "Lastly," adds the legislator, "we shall require you to pay such sums of money toward the support of these religious institutions as we may see fit to ask." "Not a farthing will you have from me," exclaims our sturdy Independent; "even did I believe in the doctrines of your church (which I do not), I should still rebel against your interference; and, if you take my property, it shall be by force and under protest."

What now does this proceeding amount to when regarded in the abstract? It amounts to an assertion by the individual of the right to exercise one of his faculties—the religious sentiment—without let or hindrance, and with no limit save that set up by the equal claims of others. And what is meant by ignoring the State? Simply an assertion of the right similarly to exercise *all* the faculties. The one is just an expansion of the other—rests on the same footing with the other—must stand or fall with the other. Men do indeed speak of civil and religious liberty as different things: but the distinction is quite arbitrary. They are parts of the same whole, and cannot philosophically be separated.

"Yes they can," interposes an objector; "assertion of the one is imperative as being a religious duty. The liberty to worship God in the way that seems to him right, is a liberty without which a man cannot fulfil what he believes to be divine commands, and therefore conscience requires him to maintain it." True enough; but how if the same can be asserted of all other liberty? How if maintenance of this also turns out to be a matter of conscience? Have we not seen that human happiness is the divine will—that only by exercising our faculties is this happiness obtainable—and that it is impossible to exercise

15

them without freedom? And, if this freedom for the exercise of faculties is a condition without which the divine will cannot be fulfilled, the preservation of it is, by our objector's own showing, a duty. Or, in other words, it appears not only that the maintenance of liberty of action *may* be a point of conscience, but that it *ought* to be one. And thus we are clearly shown that the claims to ignore the State in religious and in secular matters are in essence identical.

The other reason commonly assigned for nonconformity admits of similar treatment. Besides resisting State dictation in the abstract, the Dissenter resists it from disapprobation of the doctrines taught. No legislative injunction will make him adopt what he considers an erroneous belief; and, bearing in mind his duty toward his fellow-men, he refuses to help through the medium of his purse in disseminating this erroneous belief. The position is perfectly intelligible. But it is one which either commits its adherents to civil nonconformity also, or leaves them in a dilemma. For why do they refuse to be instrumental in spreading error? Because error is adverse to human happiness. And on what ground is any piece of secular legislation disapproved? For the same reason—because thought adverse to human happiness. How then can it be shown that the State ought to be resisted in the one case and not in the other? Will any one deliberately assert that, if a government demands money from us to aid in *teaching* what we think will produce evil, we ought to refuse it, but that, if the money is for the purpose of *doing* what we think will produce evil, we ought not to refuse it? Yet such is the hopeful proposition which those have to maintain who recognise the right to ignore the State in religious matters, but deny it in civil matters.

§ 7. The substance of this chapter once more reminds us of the incongruity between a perfect law and an imperfect State. The practicability of the principle here laid down varies directly as social morality. In a thoroughly vicious community its admission would be productive of anarchy. In a completely virtuous one its admission will be both innocuous and inevitable. Progress toward a condition of social health—a condition, that is, in which the remedial measures of legislation will no longer be needed—is progress toward a condition in which those remedial measures will be cast aside, and the authority prescribing them disregarded. The two changes are of necessity co-ordinate. That moral sense whose supremacy will make society harmonious and government unnecessary is the same moral sense which will then make each man assert his freedom even to the extent of ignoring the State—is the same moral sense which, by deterring the majority from coercing the minority, will eventually render government impossible. And, as what are merely different manifestations of the same sentiment must bear a constant ratio to each other, the tendency to repudiate governments will increase only at the same rate that governments become needless.

Let not any be alarmed, therefore, at the promulgation of the foregoing doctrine. There are many changes yet to be passed through before it can begin to exercise much influence. Probably a long time will elapse before the right to ignore the State will be generally admitted, even in theory. It will be still longer before it receives legislative recognition. And even then there will be plenty of checks upon the premature exercise of it. A sharp experience will sufficiently instruct those who may too soon abandon legal protection. Whilst, in the majority of men, there is such a love of tried arrangements, and so great a dread of experiments, that they will probably not act upon this right until long after it is safe to do so.

Anarchist Communism.

ITS AIMS AND PRINCIPLES.

Anarchism may be briefly defined as the negation of all government and all authority of man over man; Communism as the recognition of the just claim of each to the fullest satisfaction of all his needs—physical, moral, and intellectual. The Anarchist, therefore, whilst resisting as far as possible all forms of coercion and authority, repudiates just as firmly even the suggestion that he should impose himself upon others, realising as he does that this fatal propensity in the majority of mankind has been the cause of nearly all the misery and bloodshed in the world. He understands just as clearly that to satisfy his needs without contributing, to the best of his ability, his share of labour in maintaining the general well-being, would be to live at the expense of others—to become an exploiter and live as the rich drones live to-day. Obviously, then, government on the one hand and private ownership of the means of production on the other, complete the vicious circle—the present social system—which keeps mankind degraded and enslaved.

There will be no need to justify the Anarchist's attack upon *all* forms of government: history teaches the lesson he has learned on every page. But that lesson being concealed from the mass of the people by interested advocates of "law and order," and even by many Social Democrats, the Anarchist deals his hardest blows at the sophisms that uphold the State, and urges workers in striving for their emancipation to confine their efforts to the economic field.

It follows, therefore, that politically and economically his attitude is purely revolutionary; and hence arises the vilification and misrepresentation that Anarchism, which denounces all forms of social injustice, meets with in the press and from public speakers.

Rightly conceived, Anarchism is no mere abstract ideal theory of human society. It views life and social relations with eyes disillusioned. Making an end of all superstitions, prejudices, and false sentiments, it tries to see things as they really are; and without building castles in the air, it finds by the simple correlation of established facts that the grandest possibilities of a full and free life can be placed within the reach of all, once that monstrous bulwark of all our social iniquities—the State—

has been destroyed, and common property declared.

By education, by free organisation, by individual and associated resistance to political and economic tyranny, the Anarchist hopes to achieve his aim. The task may seem impossible to many, but it should be remembered that in science, in literature, in art, the highest minds are with the Anarchists or are imbued with distinct Anarchist tendencies. Even our bitterest opponents admit the beauty of our "dream," and reluctantly confess that it would be well for humanity if it were "possible." Anarchist Communist propaganda is the intelligent, organised, determined effort to realise the "dream," and to ensure that freedom and well-being for all *shall* be possible.

CPSIA information can be obtained at www.ICGtesting.com
Printed in the USA
LVOW04s1830110115

422398LV00031B/1353/P